MANY VOICES
ONE SONG

BELIEVERS
IN
AMERICA

POEMS ABOUT AMERICANS OF ASIAN AND PACIFIC ISLANDER DESCENT

BY STEVEN IZUKI   ILLUSTRATED BY BILL FUKUDA MCCOY

CHILDRENS PRESS®
CHICAGO

Dedicated to Alex and Gina

— B. F. M.

Library of Congress Cataloging--in-Publication Data

Izuki, Steven, 1954-
    Believers in America : poems about Americans of Asian and Pacific
islander descent / by Steven Izuki : illustrated by Bill Fukuda McCoy.
      p. cm. -- (Many voices, one song)
    Summary : Poems about Asian Americans such as Patsy Mink, Kristi
Yamaguchi, and Wang Laboratories founder Dr. An Wang.
    ISBN 0-516-05152-0
    1. Asian Americans--Biography--Juvenile poetry. 2. Pacific Islander
Americans--Biography--Juvenile poetry. 3. Pacific Islander Americans--
History--Juvenile poetry. 4. Asian Americans--History--Americans--poetry.
5. Children's poetry, American. [1. Asian Americans--Poetry. 2. Pacific
Islander Americans--Poetry. 3. American poetry.] I. McCoy, Bill Fukuda, ill.
II. Title. III. Series.
PS3559.Z83B45 1994
811 ' .54--dc20   94-5081
                                             CIP
                               AC

INTRODUCTION

Americans of Asian and Pacific Islander descent are often thought of as foreigners and newcomers by fellow Americans. However, a close look at American history will reveal that Asian and Pacific Islanders have been Americans for a long time. As these poems will show, Asian and Pacific Islanders have contributed significantly to the growth of North America even before the United States of America was a country.

From the first Filipinos in America who escaped from Spanish galleons, to Chinese railroad workers of the nineteenth century and modern-day business people, astronauts, and Olympic athletes of Japanese, Korean, or South Asian ancestry, Asian and Pacific Islander Americans have played a vital role in the building of our nation. Although their experiences often were difficult, they did not allow prejudice and discrimination to thwart their progress. They have helped build our nation, defend it, and lead it because they are, and have always been, *Believers in America.*

TABLE OF CONTENTS

THE FIRST FILIPINOS IN NORTH AMERICA

In the 1500s, Spain ruled the world.
It had conquered the Philippines.
With disregard for native ownership,
It claimed it for Spain's king and queen.

Spanish galleons — huge sailing ships—
Carried cargo in 1565
From the Philippines to Mexico.
Soon new products and people arrived.

Filipino woodcutters and craftsmen
Were forced to build the galleons.
Those compelled to be sailors on ships
Became the legendary "Manilamen."

Known as the best sailors in the Pacific,
"Manilamen" made up most of the crew.
Though they had built the ships and sailed them,
Like slaves, they were denied what was due.

So while galleons were docked at ports,
Such as Acapulco and New Orleans,
Many "Manilamen" risked their lives,
Escaping by whatever means.

Some men worked their way through Mexico.
Others who jumped ship swam ashore
To a land later known as Louisiana.
Now they're part of Delta region lore.

"Manilamen" started their own settlements,
Like Manila Village and St. Malo.
They were the first Asian immigrants to settle there
In North America, long ago.

The Hawaiian Islands, tops of undersea mountains,
Were first settled by Polynesians, long ago.
After Captain Cook explored Hawaii in 1778,
International interest in the islands began to unfold.

As exceptional swimmers and seamen,
Hawaiians were employed by foreigners.
This is how some Hawaiians arrived in North America
And settled there, far from their native shore.

Kings and queens once ruled the Hawaiian Islands.
In the 1800s American missionaries came.
They spread Christianity throughout the islands,
Changing forever what would have been.

After missionaries, came American settlers
Who saw opportunity in this tropical land.
Sugarcane and pineapples flourished in Hawaii,
Attracting thousands of laborers to the islands.

Workers came from China, Japan, and the Philippines,
Korea, the Pacific Islands, and some were Portuguese.
A nation of people from different countries,
Hawaii had become a mixture of all of these.

In 1893, American businessmen took control of Hawaii.
The United States government annexed it in 1898.
Native Hawaiians became U.S. citizens in 1900.
And in 1959, it became a state.

Today, Hawaii is a world-wide tourist attraction.
It lives up to its name as the "tropical paradise."
Beautiful traditions, hula dancers, and sandy beaches.
Native Hawaiians are proud of their unique way of life.

HAWAIIANS BECOME AMERICANS

They came to America in search of "Gold Mountain"
But, for many, it was mountains they moved.
Without the Chinese the transcontinental railroad
Would not have been built. That they proved.

Backbreaking work from sun-up to sun-down,
Laying heavy track, pounding in ties.
Their heroic work, instead of bringing acclaim,
Brought discrimination, hatred, and lies.

In the heat of the scorching Utah deserts,
They blasted passes through mountainsides,
Dug tunnels in the blinding snow of the Sierra Nevada,
In the end ten percent of Chinese workers died.

Though more than 10,000 workers had labored
To link the railroad in the west with the east,
What they achieved was never acknowledged.
For their labors, the Chinese were paid least.

When the transcontinental railroad was finished
At Promontory Point, May 10, 1869,
The Chinese were excluded from the celebration,
And their place in history was unfairly denied.

CHINESE RAILROAD WORKERS

ANGEL ISLAND: THE DOOR TO AMERICA

Across the Pacific Ocean they came,
Through the Golden Gate of California,
To Angel Island in San Francisco Bay —
Immigrants on their way to the U.S.A.

Detained at Angel Island, they waited,
Endlessly waited in crowded rooms
While immigration inspectors determined
Their chances of entering the United States.

Processing began with a physical exam
Followed by numerous detailed questions
To prove they were the wife, the son,
Of Chinese living in America.

"How many times a year
Did you receive letters from your father?"
"How many steps are there
From your house to the village well?"

Then relatives verified answers
While frightened immigrants waited,
Waited to hear if their answers matched
The answers of relatives in America.

Angel Island was like a prison
To immigrants seeking a new life.
Yet, when allowed into America,
They put painful memories behind them.

Those who were sent back to China,
Without the chance of a better life,
Relived the events of the long ordeal,
Imagining what might have been.

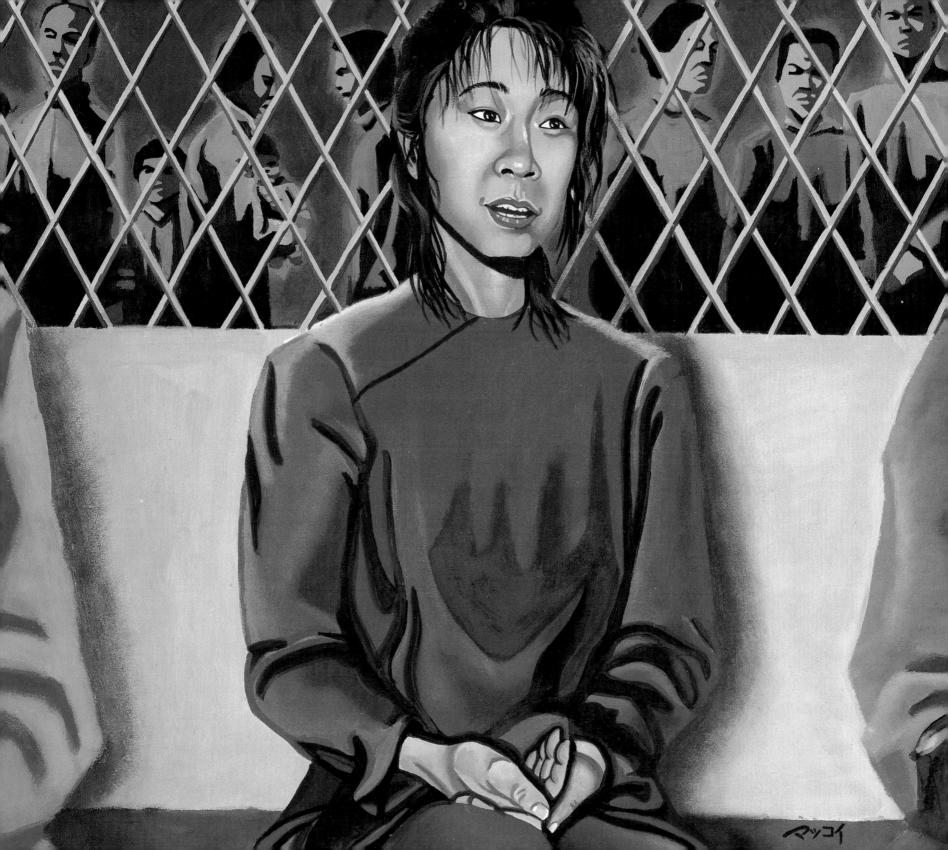

CHINESE IMMIGRANTS AND THE CHINESE EXCLUSION LAW OF 1882

Immigrants—
Their homeland China, full of strife.
So many hungry,
Always hungry.
Their destination, America
"A land," they thought, "where no one's hungry."

They came,
As laborers for a growing America
When railroads needed men
And mines needed men.
Workers to build industrial America,
Thousands were Chinese men.

Leaving behind their families,
They came.
They worked.
Harder than most they worked.
But when Americans said, "Get rid of them,
They are taking away our chances to work,"

Chinese laborers,
Who were not considered American,
Faced the Chinese Exclusion Law of 1882,
That limited Chinese immigration after 1882,
Denied families the chance to be reunited,
And denied American citizenship until 1952.

FILIPINO MIGRANT WORKERS

To America in the 1900s,
Thousands of Filipino workers came,
Believing in the American dream,
Hoping they would be rich someday.

From Alaska to California they worked,
Following jobs north and south,
Canning fish one month, picking fruit the next,
All for just a few cents in pay.

Like Japanese workers before them
And the Chinese who were first to arrive,
Filipinos worked for a piece of the dream,
But for them the dream was denied.

What they did was the most menial of jobs,
And they were paid less than those doing the same.
They faced backbreaking work, life in shantytowns,
Segregation, racism, and blame.

Filipino workers refused to give up,
Knowing they would be stronger if they stuck together.
They formed unions to demand equal pay for equal work,
Till this day the results of their unions are around.

Because of the courage of the first Filipinos,
Their children live and work everywhere in America.
Even today, when a worker is treated unfairly,
They fight on until equality can be found.

17

INTERNMENT OF JAPANESE AMERICANS

The Issei, Japanese citizens living in the United States,
Had come to America around 1900.
They wanted to work in the prosperous, new land.
America, they believed, was where a new life led.

With difficulty they adjusted to American ways,
Working hard to save money and open a business.
But "being different" and knowing very little English
Caused native workers to resent Japanese presence.

Japanese workers were insulted and picked on.
They couldn't own land and couldn't become citizens.
So they pinned their hopes on their children, the Nisei,
Who, born in America, were native citizens.

Anti-Japanese sentiments continued to persist,
Reaching a high point in December of 1941,
When Japanese planes bombed Pearl Harbor in Hawaii,
Then a new era in Japanese resentment had begun.

After the U.S. went to war with Japan,
Fear of Japanese American disloyalty spread.
Suspicion and hatred were publicly shown.
War hysteria brought racism to a head.

Politicians and newspapers declared, "The Japanese must go!"
The president issued Executive Order 9066,
Authorizing the military to evacuate all Japanese
Living on the West Coast of the United States.

In violation of their constitutional rights,
Japanese citizens lost jobs, homes, and businesses,
Were taken from schools, and imprisoned instead
In camps built in deserts and swamp areas.

Transported by train to remote camps called
Tule Lake, Poston, Heart Mountain, and Manzanar,
The Japanese would stay about three years or more
Until 1945 brought peace and an end to the war.

Patrolled by armed guards, behind barbed wire fences,
Inmates lived in rows of tar-paper barracks.
Eight to a room, no furniture, no privacy,
Owning little more than the clothes on their backs.

Not knowing how long they'd be confined,
They organized schools, clinics, and entertainment.
Newspapers were started and jobs were created
To conquer boredom and find some fulfillment.

After January 2, 1945, internment came to an end
When the government said all Japanese were free.
They could leave the camps and continue their lives
In former neighborhoods and communities.

The Japanese received little government assistance
In repairing lives destroyed by racial discrimination.
Not until the Civil Liberties Act of 1988 was passed
Was there public, mandatory reparation.

For wrongful imprisonment and loss of livelihood,
Each camp survivor received $20,000 in money.
President Reagan apologized for the "grave wrong,"
And ended "a sad chapter in American history."

When America was at war with Germany
And Japan — in World War II,
The armed services were asking for people to enlist.
Uncle Sam posters said, "I Want YOU!"

Americans of Japanese descent
Wanted to show that they were patriotic, too.
They volunteered but were quickly denied.
The army said, "We can't trust you."

The distrust was unfair and had no basis in fact,
Yet some Japanese Americans knew,
Without joining the war and giving their lives,
Their loyalty would never be proved.

As a result of their repeated petitions,
The U.S. government no longer delayed
in creating a special combat regiment
That would be made up entirely of Nisei.

From Hawaii and mainland United States,
From internment camps — everywhere it seemed —
Young Japanese Americans were volunteering
For the 100/442nd Regiment Combat Team.

They were sent overseas as a spearhead unit
Against the toughest German troops in Italy,
Fighting their way through the mountains of France,
They were some of the best soldiers in history.

After the war the soliders of the 442nd
Were all asked to come to Washington,
Where the president spoke the following words
As he honored them with a presidential citation.

"I can't tell you how much I appreciate . . .
[all the things that] you have done. . . .
You fought not only the enemy,
But you fought prejudice . . . and you won!"

THE 100/442ND REGIMENT

Daniel Inouye was born in Hawaii in 1924
And was seventeen when it was attacked by Japan.
Two years later, he enlisted in the United States army,
A young Japanese American taking a stand.

He became second lieutenant in the Nisei Regiment,
A special all-Japanese combat team,
And was given a battlefield commission in Europe
Where World War II was raging supreme!

As a platoon leader in the 100/442nd in Italy,
He fought bravely against German invaders.
He led his men through the fiercest battles,
Was wounded; his arm had to be amputated.

With honors, he returned to the United States,
An American GI of Japanese descent.
Though he wore his uniform and had medals on,
He wasn't treated as American one hundred percent.

At home, many Americans who had doubted
The loyalty of all Japanese Americans
Still showed their hatred for anyone
Whose ancestors had come from Japan.

Discrimination didn't stop Inouye
From loving his country and serving it.
He became a lawyer, then entered politics
In the Hawaiian House of Representatives.

When Hawaii became a state in 1959,
Inouye became its first U.S. representative.
Then in 1962 he entered the U.S. Senate
Where he's still serving as a Democrat.

DANIEL INOUYE, UNITED STATES SENATOR

DR. AN WANG, FOUNDER OF WANG LABORATORIES

In 1945 An Wang came from Shanghai,
From a China torn apart by war,
To study American technology.
His English and income were poor.

He attended Harvard University,
Where he earned his Master's and Ph.D.,
Then went on to discover how computers
Could store more memory.

Wang's solution to the problem of
Increasing computer information
Was to build the magnetic memory core.
Eventually it changed the whole nation.

Wang patented his revolutionary invention
And started a company of his own.
With just $600 and a small rented space,
Wang Laboratories was brilliantly born.

In the 1960s it produced electronic calculators.
In the '70s it led with word processors.
In the '80s it was office automation systems.
The company was worth billions of dollars.

Wang's success story began with an idea
And grew stronger with intelligence and determination.
His contributions ushered in the computer age.
Today it's an electronic sensation!

Korea, a peninsula south of China,
Has always been caught in the middle
When its Asian neighbors were at war.

Throughout history, it has been invaded and conquered,
Yet, each time, courageous Koreans have proven
They were stronger than before.

Hearing news that countries across the Pacific Ocean
Might offer a better life, they left their homeland,
Like the Chinese, Japanese, and Filipinos had done.

Some became plantation workers in Hawaii,
Others chose to be farmers in the United States.
All realized how far from Korea they had to come.

KOREAN AMERICANS

There were few Koreans in America until the 1950s
When American soldiers, fighting in the Korean War,
Were stationed in South Korea and married Korean women.

Returning soldiers brought their "war brides" home to the U.S.A.
And in 1952, before the Korean War had come to an end,
Korean-born immigrants were allowed to become U.S. citizens.

But not until the Immigration Act of 1965
Were Asians allowed in great numbers into the United States.
By 1970, the decade of large Korean immigration had begun.

Korean families came to start businesses of their own,
In the belief that if they worked hard, whatever they wanted to be
Is what they could successfully become.

Today, Americans of Korean descent work in every kind of job,
From owning dry-cleaning, grocery, and convenience store businesses,
To working as teachers, doctors, lawyers, and engineers.

The new generation of Korean American professionals
Is proud of the achievements of their ancestors
Whose struggles have led to successes year after year.

In the 1950s and 1960s,
Most American women remained in the home.
Not Patsy Takemoto Mink.
She boldly struck out on her own,

Attending law school, becoming a lawyer,
Then the political arena attracted her.
She supported Hawaiian workers' rights
To break free from plantation owners.

She founded the Oahu Young Democrats,
Then was elected to Hawaii's State Senate.
On to the U.S. House of Representatives,
Where she was one of the few women in it.

Patsy Mink fought for average people
And always stuck up for the poor.
In the 1960s she was called many names
For opposing the Vietnam War.

In all she served eight terms in Congress
And is still active in politics today,
Serving Hawaii's multiracial population
In a fair and loyal way.

Criticism never stops Patsy Mink
From doing what she thinks is right.
She forges ahead against all the odds,
Refusing to give up the fight!

PATSY
TAKEMOTO
MINK,
U.S. CONGRESSWOMAN

Born in America; raised in Hong Kong,
He was skilled in kung fu, his discipline strong.
Studying most of the martial arts,
He took from each some of the better parts.

From kung fu, and wing chun, and aikido,
Tai chi, and karate, and tae kwon do,
He created his famous fighting style
And presented it to Americans while

He landed a job in Hollywood
Incorporating all the skills he could.
He played sidekick Kato in "The Green Hornet,"
Thought of a TV show and hoped to star in it.

The show was a western. It was called "Kung Fu."
But when a white actor was chosen, Bruce Lee knew
He would return to Asia to be a star.
So that's what he did, and his fame spread far.

The movies followed one after the next.
In full-action films Lee was the best.
Fists of Fury, *The Chinese Connection*,
Then *Game of Death*, and *Enter the Dragon*.

In no time Lee had become a sensation,
Building a following across every nation.
His martial arts speed put fans in a daze,
Worldwide he started a martial arts craze.

Now Lee was the star he wanted to be.
It was unfortunate he died in 1973.
Although Bruce Lee is gone, his legend remains.
A martial arts master. Long live his reign!

BRUCE LEE, MARTIAL ARTIST AND ACTOR

Of the Olympic Games in London,
A story should be told
About two Asian American divers
Who won the Olympic Gold.

Korean American Sammy Lee
Had a goal. That was to win!
To prove that a person of color could be
A national diving champion.

Defying those who said it couldn't be done,
Lee won the U.S. championship in 1942,
Then finished medical school and became a doctor,
Attaining his second goal, too.

Filipino American Vicki Manalo Draves
Also joined the competitive diving mix.
She became the women's platform
(High diving) champion in 1946.

In the 1948 Olympic Games,
Lee and Draves put all they had on the line.
They showed the grace and mental toughness
That were expected of them at the time.

The first Asian American to win the gold
Was none other than Sammy Lee.
Next came Draves, who won two gold medals—
First woman diver in Olympic Games history!

Draves then became a professional swimming star,
Performing in a national Aqua Follies tour.
Lee won another gold medal for diving
At the Helsinki Olympics in 1952.

Sammy Lee served as a member of
The President's Council on Physical Fitness,
Then coached another Olympic diver,
Samoan American, Gold Medalist Greg Louganis.

VICKI MANALO DRAVES AND DR. SAMMY LEE, U. S. OLYMPIC DIVERS

WELCOME TO CHINATOWN

You might have seen where we grew up,
Most people call it Chinatown,
Our neighborhood where we live and work,
And where curious tourists abound.

My parents and cousins once lived here
'Cause they had nowhere else to go.
Wherever they looked for a job or a house,
Prejudiced people emphatically told them, "No!"

Restaurants and traditional shops
Line the streets of old Chinatown,
They've been family-owned for a very long time.
For generations they've been handed down.

Our life here is not exotic or strange.
Don't believe everything you see on TV.
We're not all bad guys eating fortune cookies.
You can bet we're not all Bruce Lee!

We don't go around saying "Confucius say,"
And we eat more than sweet 'n, sour pork.
We use chopsticks, that's true, but also
Eat our meals with a knife and a fork.

As you see, most of us speak English,
'Cause we went to the same schools as you.
We're full-blooded, patriotic Americans
Born and raised here for a century or two.

So welcome to Chinatown, our neighborhood,
A colorful mix of names and faces.
We, too, are part of the American dream,
Just trying to make a living like everyone else is.

I know you might have seen me before.
I am the owner of your corner store.
If you are wondering why I'm there,
I'll answer your question. Please don't stare!

I may not be what you're used to,
And my limited English might bother you.
Please listen to and understand
Why I had to leave my homeland.

In South Vietnam, where I once lived,
The country was at war —
Americans and South Vietnamese fighting
North Vietnamese and Viet Cong
In rice paddies and door-to-door.

After American forces left the South,
North Vietnamese troops swept down.
Those who opposed them fled with their lives
In the air or on the ground.

Some got away in 1975
On American ships and planes.
But others, like me, got left behind
To live under the North Vietnamese.

To be free, I fled from my country,
Selling all that I owned for some money.
I bribed the police and got on a small ship
On the South China Sea with my family.

The ship was horribly overloaded,
We barely kept it from going down.
For days and days we drifted along,
Desperately hoping we would be found.

Fresh water and food ran out quickly,
And seawater made us quite sick.
We had no choice but to drink it or die
From dehydration, exposure, and heat.

Close to the coast of Malaysia,
Our crowded boat capsized and sank.
Only the strong managed to swim to shore.
We were saved but had no one to thank.

Those of us who had finally made it
Were then put in a refugee camp.
We thought we had risked our lives to be free,
But around us was a barbed wire fence.

We waited for comfort, then waited some more,
And questioned what would be our fate,
Until an American family sponsored us,
And put us on a plane to the United States.

In America we finally found freedom,
But adjusting to a new land wasn't easy.
We couldn't understand the language,
And people were different than we were.

We carried on our family traditions
And helped each other get along.
Living together, like we had done in Vietnam,
Was helping us stay very strong.

But when our children learned English quickly
And with it, American ways —
"To be American is to be independent," they said —
Then at home less and less they stayed.

Our families had to pool all their money,
Something few Americans could understand,
So that we could start our own businesses
Even though they were on the worst pieces of land.

You see, that's how I and my family got here,
How I got to be the owner of this store.
You could do it, too, if you were willing to work
Sixteen hours a day, perhaps more.

When I hear the names people call me;
That I should go back to where I came from,
I think of how I struggled to get to America,
And to stay here, what I wouldn't overcome!

VIETNAMESE REFUGEES IN AMERICA

SOUTH ASIANS IN AMERICA

People from India and Pakistan,
Sri Lanka, Afghanistan, and Nepal,
Are called South Asians in America,
And have been living there for a while.

They came to the U.S.A. in large numbers
In the 1960s and 1970s
To get an American education
Or work in American companies.

Each brought a strong sense of its culture
And transplanted it in the new land,
Raising their children in traditional homes
As once they had done in their homelands.

When their children went to schools in America,
Where most students were different from them,
They began to think it would be better if they
Could, in America, quickly blend in.

Some wished they were tall, blonde, and blue-eyed.
Maybe then there'd be no questions asked.
They'd be accepted as everyone else had been.
Their future wouldn't be determined by their past.

They wouldn't have to live in two separate worlds,
One Asian — at home and away from school,
The other American— in every fashion and fad
The same — just like every other boy and girl.

Some thought "change" was the way to be accepted,
So to avoid hearing people make fun of their names,
Sujata became "Sue" and Bharat became "Brad."
They thought they'd no longer be embarrassed or shamed.

But change doesn't always bring acceptance,
And "being the same" destroys true individuality.
A myriad of colors is more beautiful than one.
Without choice no one ever feels free.

What each of us needs to learn as an American,
No matter what our ancestry happens to be,
Is that our country is a blend of many cultures
Whose strength lies in respecting its diversity.

ELLISON ONIZUKA, AEROSPACE ENGINEER

Once a young boy in Hawaii
Gazed up at the bright night sky,
Wishing for the day when he
Could travel among the stars.

Ellison Onizuka
Dreamed of being an astronaut,
Of being one of the very first men
To land on planet Mars.

Years later, after tough training
On the ground and in the air,
Onizuka achieved his dream of being
A mission specialist in space.

On January 24, 1985,
He joined the *Discovery* crew.
As the first Asian American astronaut,
He proudly took his place.

On January 28, 1986,
In a shuttle aimed at the sky,
Onizuka waited to take another trip
Past the gravity of earth.

The *Challenger* lifted off
With the crew of seven
Toward a dream and
Their destiny since birth.

Minutes into the flight
Tragedy struck.
Those who were watching
Saw something go terribly wrong.

A malfunction!
The shuttle exploded,
Killing every astronaut
The *Challenger* had brought along.

Loved ones grieved
While experts argued,
Calling the unbelievable
Turn of events very odd.

The nation sought comfort
In the president's words
That the astronauts had
"Touched the face of God."

Ellison Onizuka
Had lived his dream
Though he was never able
To explore planet Mars.

This courageous young man
Now gazes down from
The bright night sky,
For he lives among the stars.

MIDORI GOTO, CONCERT VIOLINIST

In Osaka, Japan, Midori Goto
Was playing the violin at the age of three.
By the time she was eight years old,
Her performance was called extraordinary.

Invited to come to the United States,
To New York in 1982,
Midori and her mother left Japan
To enroll Midori at the Juilliard School.

Called a "child prodigy" and a "wonder kid,"
Soon Midori played in concerts worldwide,
Then made her professional recital debut,
Taking New York's Carnegie Hall crowd in stride.

Today Midori is a master musician.
When she plays, mediocrity steps aside.
With fire in her bow and lightning-quick fingers,
She makes centuries-old classics come alive.

"I love playing," Midori says, passionately,
"It isn't like there's me and then there's the violin.
The violin is me. I love it so much .... "
No wonder Midori Goto is a great musician!

KRISTI YAMAGUCHI, U. S. OLYMPIC ICE SKATER

Up before dawn,
She was skating
Every day before school.

To be the best
Takes a lot of hard work.
No exception to the rule.

At six years old,
Kristi Yamaguchi
Was well on her way

Toward becoming
The best figure skater
In the world one day.

Scores of competitions,
Medals, awards,
National championships later,

One goal remained
For Kristi to attain
As a popular figure skater—

The Olympic Games
In Albertville, France,
The winter of 1992,

Where, up against
The world's top skaters,
Her talent she would prove.

Dancing on ice,
Spinning in the air,
Kristi was graceful but bold.

Falling down,
But getting back up,
She won the Olympic Gold!

GLOSSARY

acclaim Praise: applause.

acknowledge (ak NAW l'j) Admit to the truth of.

amputate (AM pyu tayt) To cut away from the body.

annex Take over a territory and make it part of a country, often forcibly.

arena (U REE nu) Area of interest (such as politics) in which certain activities take place.

authorize Give approval to: allow.

automation The use of a device to do automatically something once done by a human worker.

capsize Overturn.

Chinese Exclusion Law Law passed in 1882 that suspended Chinese immigration to the United States and declared those already in the country not eligible for citizenship.

citation (sy TAY sh'n) An official statement issued to honor a particular action.

commission Appointment of a member of the armed forces to the rank of officer.

compel Force.

confine Limit the movements of.

Confucius (kawn FYU sh's) Chinese philosopher who lived more than 2000 years ago.

destiny Fortune, fate.

discrimination (dis cri MU nay sh'n) unfair treatment.

disregard Lack of attention or respect.

diversity (du VUR si tee) Variety; difference.

evacuate Remove.

exclude Keep out; ban.

executive order Order issued by the president of the United States to enforce a law.

exotic (ig ZA tik) Foreign; different or unusual.

extraordinary Remarkable; beyond the ordinary.

flourish (FLU rish) Grow well.

forge ahead Move forward with a sudden increase of speed.

galleon (GAL y'n) Large three-masted sailing ship used from the fifteenth to seventeenth century, especially by Spain.

Golden Gate The narrow channel that connects the Pacific Ocean and San Francisco Bay.

grave Serious; harmful.

hysteria (his TER ee u) Uncontrolled emotion; violence.

incorporating Including.

internment Imprisonment or confinement, especially during wartime.

Issei (EE say) Japanese immigrant, especially to the United States.